Great British Food Made Simple

John Topham

LAMONA & John Topham

The Perfect Combination

John Topham

Great British Food Made Simple

Spring and summer are always times for parties and celebrations, and this year we can look forward to more than ever. With the Queen's diamond jubilee, as well as the usual bank holidays and family occasions, we've got all the excuses we need for street parties, barbecues and picnics. I've designed these recipes to help you make the most of this exciting season – whether you're entertaining friends and family at home, or joining in a larger community event.

You'll see I've included some of the classic British dishes that are making a comeback this year – from coronation chicken to simple poached salmon. Some more exotic flavours are also part of our heritage such as crispy duck salad, and there are lots more of those to try too. Wherever possible, I've used British ingredients, so you can prepare food that's grown close to home as well as made at home.

I've made the recipes using Lamona appliances – so I know you can achieve impressive results. If you don't cook very often, this summer is a great time to try your hand at some easy, appetising dishes. And if you love getting into the kitchen, you'll find plenty of inspiration here too.

Whether you're experienced or not, the Lamona range offers you a wide choice of appliances – all ready to help you enjoy the tastiest summer ever.

Have a fantastic time in the sunshine!

John Topham

Head Chef and owner, The General Tarleton

LAMONA & John Topham
The Perfect Combination

Classic Light Bites

Whether you serve them as starters or light lunches, these delicate dishes are full of fresh summer flavours. The emphasis is on seasonal ingredients, making the most of our country's outstanding produce.

Crispy Duck Salad

Crispy Duck Salad

Serves 4 30 mins preparation, 12 hours marinating, 2 hours 30 mins cooking

Ingredients
4 duck legs
450g duck or goose fat

For the dry cure marinade
¼ cinnamon stick
2 star anise
1 teaspoon coriander seeds
1 teaspoon black peppercorns
3 tablespoons sea salt
1 sprig thyme
Zest of ½ orange

For the dressing
1 clove garlic, crushed
1 teaspoon sea salt
2 tablespoons balsamic glaze
6 tablespoons olive oil

For the salad
100g bacon lardons
100g chorizo, thinly sliced
150g mixed salad leaves
50g croutons, ready made

Casserole dish with lid

To make the marinade

1. Grind the cinnamon, star anise, coriander seeds and black peppercorns in a pestle and mortar. Mix with the salt, thyme and orange zest, and rub over the duck legs.

2. Place in a dish, cover and keep in the fridge for 12 hours.

To cook the duck

1. Pre-heat the oven to 140°C/gas mark 1.

2. Under a cold tap, rinse the marinade off the duck legs and dry them thoroughly.

3. In a casserole dish, melt the duck or goose fat and submerge the duck legs in it. Cover with a layer of greaseproof paper, and place the casserole lid on top. Cook in the oven for 2 hours.

4. Leave to cool. You can do this up to a week in advance, as long as you store the duck legs in the fat.

5. Take the duck legs out of the fat, removing as much fat as possible. Heat a heavy-based pan and put the legs in, skin side down. Cook for 5-7 minutes until crisp and golden, then cook for a further 10 minutes in the oven.

To make the salad and serve

1. Combine the dressing ingredients in a jam jar, tighten the lid and shake well.

2. In a frying pan, crisp the bacon lardons, then the chorizo, and keep warm.

3. Divide the leaves between 4 plates, and scatter with the croutons, lardons and chorizo, then lightly toss.

4. Take the duck legs from the oven and place one on each salad.

5. Drizzle the dressing on top.

Crab Cakes

Crab Cakes

Lightly spicy and crisply fried, they make a satisfying starter, lunch or supper dish.

Serves 4 45 mins preparation, 10 mins cooking

Ingredients
2 tablespoons mayonnaise
2 tablespoons coriander, chopped
½ teaspoon madras curry powder
1 egg, lightly beaten
100g breadcrumbs, plus 2-3 tablespoons
Juice of ½ lemon
450g fresh white crab meat (ensure there are no fragments of shell)
Sea salt and milled black pepper
200ml rapeseed oil

To serve
Lime wedges and coriander leaves

1. In a large bowl, mix the mayonnaise, coriander, curry powder, egg, 100g breadcrumbs and lemon juice.

2. Fold in the crab meat and season with a little salt and pepper. If the mixture is very wet, you may need to add one more tablespoon of breadcrumbs. Cover and refrigerate for 20 minutes.

3. Divide the crab mixture into 8 round cakes and coat in breadcrumbs. Refrigerate until required.

4. Heat the oil in a non-stick frying pan over a medium heat. Once hot, cook 4 of the cakes at a time, for 2-3 minutes on each side until golden. Drain on kitchen paper and repeat with the remaining crab cakes. Serve with lime wedges and coriander leaves.

New Season Asparagus Rolled in Parma Ham

New Season Asparagus Rolled in Parma Ham

When British asparagus is in season, in May and June, its intense, fresh flavour is way beyond anything you'll taste during the rest of the year. So this simple recipe is all you need, using salty Parma ham to bring out the best in this wonderful vegetable.

Serves 4 20 mins preparation, 10 mins cooking

Ingredients
20 thick asparagus spears
1 teaspoon table salt
Bowl of iced water
10 slices Parma ham
2 tablespoons virgin olive oil
1 lemon
Milled black pepper

1. Carefully peel the asparagus spears and trim the ends.

2. Bring a large pan of salted water to the boil and have the bowl of iced water ready.

3. Blanch 10 of the asparagus spears by boiling for 2-3 minutes, depending on thickness. Then put them straight into the iced water to chill as quickly as possible. Repeat with the remaining 10 spears.

4. Drain the spears and dry them on kitchen paper.

5. Cut each slice of Parma ham in half lengthways, then roll and wrap each asparagus spear in it, leaving the tip showing. Chill them in the fridge until you're ready to finish cooking.

6. Heat a griddle pan until it's smoking hot. Brush each wrapped asparagus spear with a little olive oil and sear on both sides for 1-2 minutes.

7. Serve with a squeeze of lemon and a little black pepper.

Potted Shrimps

This traditional British dish has made a comeback in recent years – and if you try this recipe, you'll see why. The gentle spices match the richness of the shrimps perfectly, in a complex marriage of flavours.

Serves 6 25 mins preparation

Ingredients
175g unsalted butter
½ teaspoon sea salt
1 teaspoon cayenne pepper
1 teaspoon ground mace
1 pinch nutmeg
350g brown shrimps, peeled
Juice of ½ lemon

To serve
Toast or crusty bread

6 small ramekin dishes

1. Place 100g of the butter in a small saucepan. Add the salt, cayenne, mace and nutmeg and heat gently.

2. Fold in the shrimps, add the lemon juice, and warm for 2 minutes over a medium heat.

3. Divide the shrimp mixture between the ramekin dishes, pressing it down with the back of a spoon. Put the dishes in the fridge to cool.

4. In a clean pan, melt the remaining butter, and spoon it over the tops of the dishes to seal them. Chill them in the fridge until you need them.

5. Serve with plenty of toast or crusty bread.

Chilled Melon, Cucumber and Mint Soup

If you want something to cool you down on a warm day, soup might not be your first thought. But this one is amazingly refreshing – and all it takes is a quick blast in the food processor.

Serves 6 10 mins preparation

Ingredients
1 large, ripe honeydew melon
2 cucumbers
20 mint leaves

1. Peel and de-seed the melon and cucumber, and chop roughly.

2. Place in a food processor, add the mint leaves, and blend until smooth.

3. Pass the soup through a fine sieve and serve chilled.

Chilled Melon, Cucumber and Mint Soup

Great British Mains

For dinner parties and family meals, these recipes combine all kinds of spring and summer flavours. If the weather's good, you won't want to spend hours in the kitchen, so it's all about keeping things simple – but very, very tasty.

Peppered Steak

Peppered Steak

Juicy fillet steak, generously seasoned with pepper and drizzled with a rich, meaty Cognac reduction. I can't think of a better way to keep your dinner guests happy.

Serves 4 10 mins preparation, 20 mins cooking

Ingredients
4 175g fillet steaks (see my guide to choosing steak on page 22)
2 tablespoons white peppercorns
2 tablespoons black peppercorns
2 tablespoons olive oil
1 pinch sea salt
75g unsalted butter
2 splashes Cognac
2 tablespoons reduced beef stock (optional)

To serve
Chips and a green salad

1. At least 30 minutes before you start cooking, take the steaks out of the fridge to bring to room temperature.

2. Crush the peppercorns coarsely in a pestle and mortar. Tip them into a sieve and shake it to discard the dust.

3. Roll the fillets over the peppercorns, lightly pressing them into the steaks.

4. Rub olive oil onto the steaks and season with the sea salt.

5. Heat a heavy-bottomed frying pan until it's smoking, add the steaks and fry until you have a good, thick crust on both sides. You may need to reduce the heat a little at this stage to prevent burning.

6. Add 50g of the butter, turn the steaks and finish cooking them to suit your taste. Baste with the buttery juices as you go.

7. Remove the steaks from the pan, and let them rest on a warm plate for 5-10 minutes while you finish the sauce.

8. Reheat the pan, add the Cognac and let it boil for a minute to cook out the alcohol. Add the stock (optional) and whisk in the remaining butter.

9. Bring the sauce to the boil and pour over the steaks. Serve with chips and a green salad.

A guide to choosing and cooking steak

Where to buy your steak
Always buy from a good butcher, who sells the best local, traditional British breeds.

What to look for
The tastiest, juiciest steak has a light marbling of fat throughout the meat. It should be a dark red wine colour – not bright red, as you often see in supermarkets. If possible, ask for steak that's dry aged for at least 21 days.

Which type of steak
Fillet is the best for tenderness, but doesn't always have the most flavour.

Sirloin gives you a good balance of flavour and tenderness.

Rump has lots of flavour, but can be a bit chewy.

Rib-eye is both flavoursome and tender. A large rib-eye steak for two, cooked on the bone, is probably the best steak ever!

How to cook your steak
- The aim is to get a good char on the outside, while keeping the meat juicy and tender on the inside.
- Always bring your steaks up to room temperature before you cook them – keep them out of the fridge for 30-60 minutes.
- Rub a teaspoon of oil over your steak, then season with ground pepper and a mix of sea and smoked salt.
- Heat a griddle or heavy-bottomed frying pan until it's smoking hot. If you're barbecuing, wait until the flames have died down and the coals are white hot.
- Add the steaks and don't be tempted to turn them too early, as this stops the crunchy crust forming. If there's a thick layer of fat on the edge of the steak, use a pair of tongs to hold it on its side in the pan to brown the fat.
- Turn the steak and cook it to your liking (see below), then rest it in a warm place for 5-10 minutes before serving.

From rare to well done...
Cooking steak precisely to your liking can take a bit of practice. Here's a rough guide to get you started, but the results you get will depend on the thickness of the steak.

Rare: cook for 3-4 minutes on each side. The steak will feel soft and fleshy when you press it.

Medium rare: cook for 5-6 minutes on each side. The steak will resist a little when you press it.

Medium: cook for 7-8 minutes on each side. The steak will still have a little give when you press it.

Well done: cook for 10 minutes on each side. The steak will feel firm when you press it.

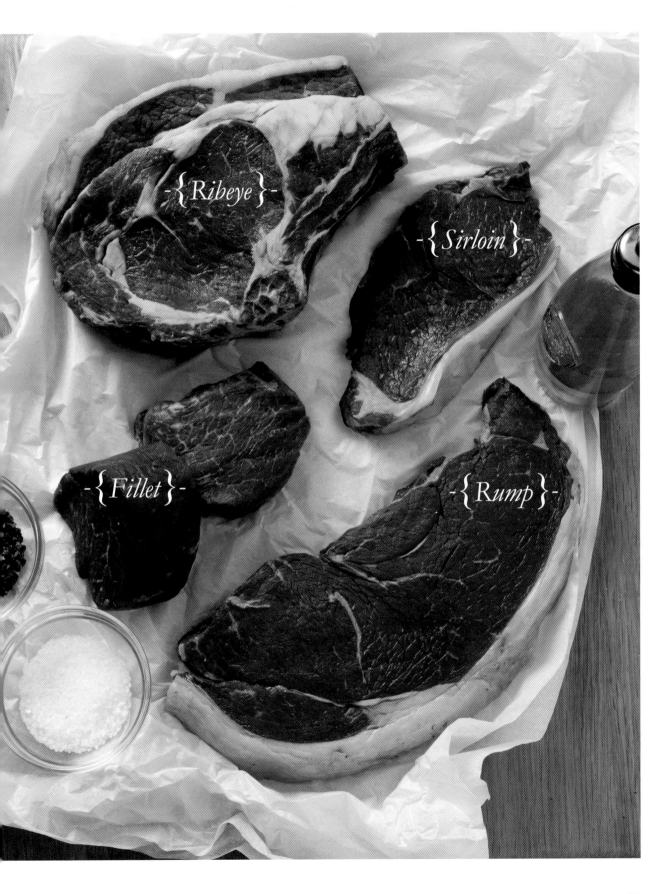

-{ Ribeye }-

-{ Sirloin }-

-{ Fillet }-

-{ Rump }-

Roast Leg of Spring Lamb and Boulangère Potatoes

The new season's lamb needs only very simple cooking with rosemary and garlic to bring out its sweet, delicate flavour. It works perfectly with classic boulangère potatoes – and I've kept the gravy simple too, letting those delicious roasting juices work their magic.

Serves 6-8 30 mins preparation, 1 hour 45 mins cooking

Ingredients

1 leg spring lamb on the bone (ask your butcher to knock the tip of the shank off to help with carving and for great presentation)
2 tablespoons olive oil
½ bulb garlic, peeled and cut into thin strips
Small bunch rosemary
Sea salt
Milled black pepper
2 tablespoons plain flour
¾ pint boiling water

For the Boulangère Potatoes

500ml stock (lamb, beef or chicken)
35g unsalted butter
1.5kg Desiree potatoes, peeled and thinly sliced
2 small onions, peeled and thinly sliced
1 teaspoon picked thyme leaves
Sea salt and milled black pepper

Large oven proof dish

1. Pre-heat the oven to 200°C/gas mark 6.

2. Rub the leg of lamb with olive oil. Using a sharp knife, make incisions into the skin of the lamb and press a slice of garlic and a small sprig of rosemary into each incision.

3. Place in a roasting tin and sprinkle with salt and pepper. Roast for 30 minutes.

4. Whilst the lamb is cooking, place the stock in a pan, bring to the boil and leave to stand. Grease the base and edges of the oven-proof dish using half the butter. Arrange the potatoes, overlapping slightly to cover the base of the dish. Sprinkle with a thin layer of onions and thyme leaves. Season with a little salt and pepper. Repeat the process and finish with a layer of potatoes on the top. Pour the stock over and dot the remaining butter on top.

5. Reduce the heat to 180°C/gas mark 4, cover the lamb with tin foil to protect the rosemary from burning and place the potatoes in the oven.

6. Carry on cooking for 1 hour. Remove from the oven and place the lamb on a suitable dish to rest in a warm place.

7. To make the gravy, remove the excess fat from the roasting tin and place in a bowl, leaving the roasting juices in the tin. Add the flour to the bowl and mix it into a smooth paste.

8. Add the boiling water to the roasting juices and mix well over a low heat. Once it is boiling, thicken by whisking in the flour paste a little at a time.

9. Cook for a further 2 minutes. Place the lamb on top of the potatoes and gravy on the side to serve.

Roast Leg of Spring Lamb and Boulangère Potatoes

Roast Spring Chicken

By 'spring chicken' we usually mean a young one, with very tender meat. This easy recipe brings out the best in any good quality chicken, keeping it beautifully moist on the inside while making the outside deliciously crisp.

Serves 5-6 10 mins preparation, 1 hour 15 mins cooking

Ingredients
1 lemon, juice and grated zest (save the lemon halves)
Sea salt and milled black pepper
100g unsalted butter at room temperature
1.8kg free range chicken
2 cloves garlic, crushed
1 small bunch fresh thyme
1 tablespoon plain flour
300ml boiling water

To serve
Spring vegetables or salad
New potatoes

1. Pre-heat the oven to 220°C/gas mark 8.

2. Mix the lemon zest with a pinch of sea salt and put to one side.

3. Using your hands, smear the butter all over the chicken and place it in a roasting tin. Season with the pepper and squeeze the lemon juice over.

4. Put the squeezed-out lemon halves, garlic and thyme inside the chicken cavity.

5. Roast the chicken for 15 minutes. Baste it with the juices, then turn the oven down to 190°C/gas mark 5 and roast for 40 minutes more, basting occasionally.

6. Sprinkle the salted lemon zest over the chicken and cook for a further 10 minutes. Remove it from the oven – it should be golden brown and crisp.

7. Lift and tip the chicken to let the juices run from the cavity back into the roasting tin. Place the chicken on a dish and keep in a warm place for 15 minutes before carving.

8. Pour 2 tablespoons of the roasting juices into a cup, mix with the flour and blend to a smooth paste. Add the boiling water to the roasting tin and, over a medium heat, whisk in the flour paste to thicken, and then simmer for 2 minutes.

9. Carve the chicken, and serve with spring vegetables or salad, and new potatoes.

Roast Spring Chicken

Pan Roast Monkfish with Spring Onion Potato Cakes

Pan Roast Monkfish with Spring Onion Potato Cakes

Serves 4 30 mins preparation, 40 mins cooking

Ingredients

200g unsalted butter
8 spring onions
4 medium potatoes
Sea salt and milled black pepper
2 tablespoons plain flour

700g monkfish fillet, trimmed and divided into 4
2 tablespoons olive oil
Juice of 1 lemon
150ml crème fraîche
1 dessert spoon ground cumin
Small packet of rocket leaves

1. Pre-heat the oven to 140°C/gas mark 1.

2. Start by clarifying the butter. To do this, melt it gently in a pan, then leave it to settle and scoop off any solids that form on the surface. Carefully ladle the clear melted butter into a bowl, discarding the milky residue that is left behind.

3. Prepare the spring onions by peeling off any tired outer leaves, then cut them lengthways into fine strips.

4. Peel the potatoes and grate onto a clean tea towel. Wrap the towel around the grated potato and squeeze it firmly over the sink to remove as much starch as possible.

5. Heat a medium frying pan and add 3 tablespoons of the clarified butter, then half the grated potatoes. Using a spoon, gently press the potato into a flat, round shape. Season with salt and pepper, spread the spring onions over, and cover with the remaining potato.

6. Cook gently for 8-10 minutes until the bottom is browned. You should hear the potatoes sizzling, so if they get too dry, add more clarified butter. Turn the potato cake by carefully sliding it onto a plate and flipping it over, back into the pan. Add more clarified butter if necessary and cook on that side for another 8-10 minutes until brown.

7. Transfer the potato cake onto a wire rack over a baking sheet, and keep it warm in the oven while you cook the monkfish.

8. Heat a large frying pan over a medium heat. Put the flour on a small plate and season with salt and pepper. Dust each piece of monkfish with the flour.

9. Add 1 tablespoon of olive oil and 2 tablespoons of clarified butter to the pan. Carefully place the monkfish in the pan and cook for 2-3 minutes on each side, until golden.

10. When it's cooked, squeeze half of the lemon juice over it, then keep it warm in the oven with the potato cake.

11. In a small bowl, mix the crème fraîche, remaining lemon juice and cumin.

12. Divide the potato cake into four. Place each piece onto a small bunch of rocket in the centre of the plate. Set the monkfish on top, drizzle with the pan juices and serve with the crème fraîche mixture.

Sweet Potato and Goats' Cheese Tarts

Whether you're a vegetarian or not, the combination of mellow sweet potato and fresh goats' cheese – all lightly spiced in a melting pastry tart – makes a satisfying summer main course.

Serves 4 30 mins preparation, 1 hour 15 mins cooking

Ingredients

1kg sweet potatoes
250g ready made puff pastry
120ml soured cream
1 dessert spoon ground cumin seeds
Sea salt and milled black pepper
100g goats' cheese

2 tablespoons pumpkin seeds
1 medium hot chilli, finely chopped
2 tablespoons olive oil
1 garlic clove, crushed
1 tablespoon flat-leaf parsley, chopped

1. Pre-heat the oven to 200°C/gas mark 6.

2. Bake the sweet potatoes in their skins for 45 minutes. Leave them to cool until you can handle them, then peel them and cut into 5mm slices.

3. On a lightly floured work surface, roll out the puff pastry until it's 2mm thick. Cut it into 4 rectangles and prick it all over with a fork. Place it on a baking tray lined with baking parchment, and rest in the fridge for 30 minutes.

4. Mix together the soured cream and ground cumin seeds.

5. Remove the pastry from the fridge. Spread a thin layer of the soured cream mixture over each rectangle, leaving a 5mm border around each one.

6. Arrange the sweet potato slices on each piece of pastry, and season with salt and pepper.

7. Crumble the goats' cheese on top, and sprinkle with pumpkin seeds and chilli.

8. Bake for 20-25 minutes.

9. While the tarts are cooking, mix the olive oil, garlic, parsley and a pinch of salt. As soon as the tarts come out of the oven, brush them with the oil mixture. Serve warm or at room temperature.

Sweet Potato and Goats' Cheese Tarts

Puddings and Baking

Lighter, fruitier desserts always go down well in summer, but a little indulgence is very welcome too. These puds combine the best of both worlds, giving you and your guests a wonderful treat at the end of the meal.

Summer Pudding

Summer Pudding

Of all the seasonal summer recipes, I think this is the most characteristically British – with all those fruits we grow so well here. It's deliciously tangy as well as sweet, so fresh cream goes perfectly with it.

Serves 6 20 mins preparation, 12 hours setting

Ingredients
1kg mixed fresh or frozen berries (such as raspberries, strawberries, blackberries, blackcurrants, blueberries and redcurrants)
250g caster sugar
150ml water (only if you're using fresh berries)
8 slices white bread, slightly stale

To serve
Double or clotted cream

1½ pint pudding basin

1. In a large saucepan, bring the berries and caster sugar (and water if you're using fresh berries) gently to the boil, and simmer for a few minutes. Remove from the heat.

2. Cut the crusts off the bread and dip one side of each slice into the warm fruits.

3. Starting at the base and then working up the sides, line the pudding basin with each slice, dipped side facing outwards.

4. When the basin is fully lined, use a slotted spoon to fill it with the berries. Leave enough room for a bread lid, and place this on top.

5. Put the pudding basin on a deep-rimmed plate to catch any juices. Place a saucer on top of the bread lid, and keep it in the fridge for 12 hours to set.

6. Pass the remaining fruit through a fine sieve to make a coulis, and keep it in the fridge until you need it.

7. To serve the pudding, remove the saucer, and carefully run a knife around the rim of the basin. Put a plate on top, and hold it in place as you turn the basin upside down. Carefully lift away the basin, letting the pudding slide out onto the plate. Cover with the fruit coulis and serve with double or clotted cream.

Peach Melba

This classic summer dessert is an exuberant marriage of flavours and colours. Poaching the peaches in syrup really intensifies the taste, and the raspberry tang livens it up perfectly.

Serves 4 30 mins preparation

Ingredients
2 fresh, ripe peaches
150g caster sugar
275ml white wine
175g fresh raspberries

To serve
1 tub good quality vanilla ice cream

1. Bring a pan of water to the boil, drop in the peaches and blanch for 10-12 seconds.

2. Lift them out and leave to cool, then peel off the skins. Cut them in half, remove the stones, and set aside.

3. Bring the sugar and white wine to the boil, add the peach halves and poach gently for 10 minutes. Leave to cool in the syrup before lifting out onto a dish.

4. Bring the syrup back to the boil and reduce by half.

5. In a food blender, purée the raspberries and syrup, then pass through a fine sieve into a bowl. Chill in the fridge.

6. Using 4 small serving dishes, place a large scoop of vanilla ice cream on each plate with a peach half and pour over the raspberry purée.

Peach Melba

New York Cheesecake

New York Cheesecake

Serves 8 30 mins preparation, 1 hour 15 mins cooking, 6 hours cooling

Ingredients
For the Base
65g unsalted butter, plus 20g to grease the cake tin
250g digestive biscuits

For the Filling
450g full fat cream cheese at room temperature
225g mascarpone cheese
100g caster sugar
1 vanilla pod
4 large eggs

2 large egg yolks
1 teaspoon lemon juice
75ml double cream
Grated zest of 1 lemon
Grated zest of 1 orange

22-24cm springform cake tin, 5-6cm deep
Deep-sided roasting tin

To make the base

1. Pre-heat the oven to 180°C/gas mark 4.

2. Grease the cake tin with 20g of the butter. Crush the digestive biscuits in a food processor, to make crumbs. Melt 65g of the butter and mix it with the biscuit crumbs.

3. Tip the biscuit mixture into the cake tin, and spread it to create an even layer, pressing down firmly. Bake for 12 minutes until firm, then set aside to cool.

To make the filling

1. Reduce the oven to 170°C/gas mark 3.

2. Put the cake tin onto a double layer of foil, large enough to come up to the rim. Bring the foil up the sides, then put the cake tin in the roasting tin – this will make a water bath.

3. Using an electric mixer fitted with a paddle, combine the cream cheese, mascarpone and sugar, and beat at a low speed before increasing to a medium speed. Beat for 3-4 minutes, scraping down the sides as necessary until you have a light, smooth mixture.

4. Split the vanilla pod lengthways and scrape out the seeds.

5. In a small bowl, use a fork to lightly beat the eggs, egg yolks and vanilla seeds. Add the lemon juice, then slowly add the egg mixture to the cream cheese mixture, beating until smooth. Slowly pour in the cream, and finally stir in the lemon and orange zest. Pour the finished mixture on top of the biscuit base.

6. Make the water bath by pouring boiling water into the roasting tin, outside of the cake tin, up to halfway up the cake tin.

7. Bake for 1 hour until the cheesecake has set and is a light, golden brown. Remove the cheesecake from the oven and leave to cool in the water bath until it reaches room temperature.

8. Take the cheesecake out of the water bath, keeping it in the tin. Chill in the fridge for at least 6 hours.

9. Remove the tin from the fridge, release and remove the sides, and cut the cheesecake into slices. Serve with summer fruits.

Victoria Sponge Cake

When it comes to baking, the simplest recipes are often the best – and this takes some beating. Using whipped cream as well as jam in the filling transforms this tea-time treat into an indulgent dessert.

Serves 10 15 mins preparation, 55 mins cooking, plus cooling

Ingredients
175g self-raising flour, sifted
175g unsalted butter, softened
175g caster sugar
3 large eggs, beaten
2 level teaspoons baking powder
2 drops vanilla essence
3 tablespoons milk

For the filling
250ml double cream
3 tablespoons raspberry jam (see page 90 for my recipe)
1 dessert spoon icing sugar, sifted

20cm cake tin

1. Pre-heat the oven to 170°C/gas mark 3.

2. Line the cake tin with greaseproof paper and grease.

3. Put all the ingredients, apart from the milk, into a large bowl and beat (slowly at first) for 2 minutes. An electric mixer is ideal for this.

4. Stir in enough milk to give you a soft consistency that drops off a spoon.

5. Spoon the mixture into the cake tin, and bake for 50-55 minutes until the cake has risen. To check it's cooked, insert a skewer into the centre of the cake – it should come out clean.

6. Leave the cake to cool for a few minutes, and then turn it out onto a wire rack to finish cooling.

7. When it's cool, carefully slice the cake horizontally in two.

8. Whip the cream into soft peaks. Spread the raspberry jam evenly onto the bottom half of the cake, followed by the cream. Carefully replace the top half, and dust the top with sifted icing sugar.

Victoria Sponge Cake

Lemon Drizzle Cake

Lemon Drizzle Cake

With its moist, sweet sponge, fresh lemon flavour and crisp, sugary topping, this cake is always a family favourite. It's lovely by itself, but also makes a great pudding with a dollop of cream or crème fraîche.

Serves 10 25 mins preparation, 40 mins cooking

Ingredients
125g butter
175g caster sugar
2 lemons, juice and grated zest
2 eggs, beaten
175g self-raising flour
75g icing sugar

To decorate
Zest of ½ lemon

20cm cake tin

1. Pre-heat the oven to 180°C/gas mark 4.
2. Line the cake tin with greaseproof paper.
3. Mix the butter and caster sugar together in a large bowl.
4. Add the lemon zest, then the eggs a little at a time, beating thoroughly after each addition.
5. Sift the self-raising flour, and fold into the mixture.
6. Pour the mixture into the cake tin, and bake for 40 minutes until golden. To check it's cooked, insert a skewer into the centre of the cake – it should come out clean.
7. Leave the cake in the tin to cool.
8. Make the drizzling syrup by heating the lemon juice and icing sugar gently in a small pan, until the sugar has dissolved.
9. Use a cocktail stick to prick holes all over the surface of the cake, and then pour on the hot syrup, allowing it to soak into the holes.
10. Let the cake cool in the tin to ensure it absorbs all the syrup before you serve it. Decorate with lemon zest shavings.

Summer Party Celebrations

If you're getting together with neighbours, you'll want tables groaning with
crowd-pleasing favourites – and here you have everything you need. You can
also serve these at smaller celebrations. So let's get the party started!

Coronation Chicken

Coronation Chicken

As this dish was invented for the Queen's coronation, it seems apt to recreate it in her diamond jubilee year. But you don't really need that excuse, as it's delicious at any time.

Serves 6 40 mins preparation, 1 hour cooking

Ingredients

1 whole chicken
4 cloves
2 bay leaves
1 carrot, chopped
2 onions, chopped
2 cloves garlic, finely chopped
1 tablespoon olive oil
½ lemon, sliced
3 dessert spoons curry powder

150ml white wine
1 heaped tablespoon mango chutney
400g mayonnaise
Sea salt and milled black pepper
50g raisins
20g toasted flaked almonds
Coriander leaves for garnish

1. Place the chicken in a large pan and cover with cold water. Add the cloves, bay leaves, carrot and one of the onions. Bring to a simmer and cook gently for 1 hour, then leave the chicken to cool in the stock.

2. In a large frying pan, gently fry the remaining onion and the garlic in the olive oil until they're soft and opaque. Add the lemon and curry powder, cook for a further 2 minutes, and then add the white wine.

3. Bring to the boil, reducing the sauce a little. Add the mango chutney and leave to cool.

4. Discard the lemon slices and liquidise the sauce. Whisk in the mayonnaise and taste to check if it needs a little salt and pepper.

5. Remove the chicken from the stock pan, take off the skin, and pull the meat off in bite-sized pieces, placing into a serving dish.

6. Add the sauce and mix well. Sprinkle with the raisins and toasted almonds, and garnish with coriander leaves.

Poached Salmon

In this recipe, you use a court bouillon – a lightly spiced, aromatic broth – to poach the fish. This gives it much more flavour than just cooking it in water, and takes only a few minutes to prepare.

Serves 8 20 mins preparation, 1 hour cooking

Ingredients
1.5kg whole piece of salmon on the bone

For the Court Bouillon
1 onion, peeled and roughly chopped
1 celery stick, halved
1 carrot, halved
6 peppercorns
4 cloves
2 bay leaves
2 tablespoons white wine vinegar
1 teaspoon sea salt

To serve
Salad and mayonnaise

Greaseproof paper

1. Cut a rectangular piece of greaseproof paper to use as a sling to help lift the salmon out of the pan when it's cooked. It needs to be large enough to support the salmon and wide enough for you to hold either end.

2. Put all the ingredients for the court bouillon into a large pan. Lay the greaseproof sling on top, followed by the salmon, and cover with cold water.

3. Bring to a simmer and cook for 3 minutes. Turn off the heat, cover with a lid and leave for 40-50 minutes.

4. When it's cool, carefully lift the salmon out of the pan in the sling, and onto a tray.

5. Remove the skin by slipping a sharp, pointed knife along the backbone and carefully peeling the skin away.

6. Using the back of the knife, remove the dark flesh by sliding your knife away from the tail end.

7. Carefully insert the knife down the natural centre line, and lift the salmon flesh away from the bone and onto a serving plate. Try to keep each side in one piece.

8. Serve the salmon cold, with salad and mayonnaise.

Poached Salmon

Fillet of Beef Salad

When you're celebrating outdoors, a luxurious salad of fillet beef, dressed with a horseradish cream and parmesan shavings, makes an impressive centrepiece.

Serves 6 25 mins preparation, 10 mins cooking

Ingredients
750g beef fillet, trimmed
100ml olive oil
1 teaspoon sea salt
Milled black pepper
2 dessert spoons creamed horseradish
3 tablespoons crème fraîche
200g baby beetroot, cooked
Small bunch rocket
Small bunch watercress
100g parmesan, peeled into shavings
2 tablespoons capers

1. Heat a griddle pan or heavy-bottomed frying pan until it's smoking hot. Rub 2 tablespoons of olive oil over the fillet, and season with the salt and a lot of pepper.

2. Seal the fillet in the pan for 2 minutes on each side. Leave to cool.

3. In a small bowl, mix the horseradish and crème fraîche until smooth.

4. Slice the beef thinly and arrange on a large serving platter. Dot the beetroot around, and scatter with the rocket and watercress leaves. Drizzle with the horseradish cream mixture, and scatter the parmesan shavings over the top.

5. Heat the remaining olive oil in a frying pan. When it's hot, fry the capers for 40-50 seconds, drain on kitchen paper and scatter over the platter.

Summer Vegetable Tart

Summer Vegetable Tart

Combining courgettes, onion and celery with two cheeses and pine nuts gives you a savoury tart with bags of flavour and a satisfying texture. Try it as a lunchtime main course, or in a party buffet.

Serves 6 30 mins preparation, 50 mins cooking

Ingredients

For the Pastry
50g cold butter, diced
50g lard or solid vegetable oil, diced
175g plain flour
1 egg yolk
4 tablespoons cold water
1 pinch table salt

23cm loose bottom quiche tin

For the Filling
30g pine nuts
A little olive oil
40g mature cheddar cheese
40g gruyere cheese
1 medium courgette
1 small onion, finely chopped
1 celery stalk, finely chopped
2 eggs, beaten
300ml double cream
1 teaspoon English mustard
Sea salt and milled black pepper

To make the pastry

1. Pre-heat the oven to 190°C/gas mark 5.

2. Put the butter and lard (or solid vegetable oil) into a food processor along with the other ingredients and pulse until the mixture binds together. Alternatively, use your fingertips to rub the butter and lard lightly through the flour, until the mixture resembles breadcrumbs, then add enough of the water to bind together.

3. Turn the pastry out onto a lightly floured board. Gather it into a ball and roll it out.

4. Line the quiche tin with the pastry, and chill it in the fridge for 10 minutes.

5. Cover the pastry snugly with a sheet of tin foil and bake for 10 minutes. Carefully remove the foil and bake for a further 5 minutes.

To make the filling

1. Fry the pine nuts in a little olive oil, until they're slightly brown.

2. Grate the cheeses and courgette into a bowl and add the pine nuts, onion and celery.

3. Combine the eggs, cream and mustard, and season with salt and pepper. Mix this with the other ingredients and pour into the pastry case.

4. Bake in the oven for 30-35 minutes, until golden and just firm. Serve warm or cold.

Homemade Sausage Rolls

Using ready-made pastry speeds up your preparation time – and you can still get all those exciting homemade flavours into your filling.

Makes 8 1 hour preparation, 20 mins cooking

Ingredients
320g pack of pre-rolled puff pastry
1 egg, beaten (for glazing)

For the filling
250g minced pork
250g sausage meat
1 small onion, very finely chopped
2 tablespoons tomato ketchup
2 tablespoons brown sauce
1 dessert spoon Worcestershire sauce
1 tablespoon thyme leaves
1 tablespoon sage, finely chopped
Sea salt and milled black pepper

Non-stick baking parchment

1. Combine and mix all the filling ingredients together.

2. Cut the sheet of pastry lengthways into 2 long rectangles. With a rolling pin, carefully roll the pastry to make it a little wider, then put one half to the side.

3. Spoon half the filling mixture along the pastry, leaving a small margin at the top. Spread the mixture evenly in a sausage shape, so it reaches the edges of the pastry on the left and right sides. Roll the pastry tightly over the filling from left to right to make a big, long sausage roll. Brush the edges with the beaten egg and seal.

4. Repeat the process with the other half of the pastry and the rest of the filling.

5. Wrap the long sausage rolls in cling film and place in the fridge for at least 30 minutes.

6. Pre-heat the oven to 200°C/gas mark 6.

7. Line a baking tray with non-stick baking parchment.

8. Remove the sausage rolls from the fridge, and take off the cling film. Cut each length into 4, brush with the beaten egg and place on the baking tray. Bake for 20 minutes until lightly browned.

Homemade Sausage Rolls

Pavlova

Pavlova

Perfect for a summer party, this dessert is easier to put together than you might think, as the meringue just needs forming into a simple nest shape.

Serves 6 20 mins preparation, 1 hour cooking

Ingredients
3 large egg whites
1 teaspoon cornflour
175g caster sugar
1 teaspoon malt vinegar
Few drops vanilla essence
275ml double cream
350g assorted berries

Non-stick baking parchment

1. Pre-heat the oven to 150°C/gas mark 2.

2. Line a baking sheet with non-stick baking parchment (I find this works better than greaseproof paper for this recipe).

3. Place the egg whites in a large clean bowl, then whisk them with an electric whisk until they form stiff peaks – you should be able to turn the bowl upside down without them moving.

4. Add the cornflour to the sugar, then add this to the egg whites – a teaspoon at a time, whisking after each addition – until it's all mixed in.

5. Add the vinegar and vanilla essence to the mixture, and fold in lightly with a tablespoon.

6. Spoon just over half of the meringue mixture onto the baking sheet, and spread it into a circle, about 18cm in diameter, to make the base.

7. To form the sides of the pavlova, add the remaining mixture, a tablespoon at a time, around the edge of the circle. Use a fork to shape the sides, so it resembles a nest.

8. Bake the pavlova for 1 hour. Remove it from the oven when it looks set, then leave it to cool completely.

9. When it's cold, lift it carefully from the baking sheet. Peel off the baking parchment and place the pavlova on a serving plate.

10. When you're ready to serve, whip the cream and spread it in the centre of the pavlova, arranging the fruit on top.

Pimms Jelly and Summer Punch

Pimms Jelly

Serves 6-8 1 hour preparation, plus setting time

Ingredients

600ml lemonade
250ml Pimms
400g sugar
Juice of 1 lemon

12 leaves gelatine
½ cucumber
1 granny smith apple
1 pink grapefruit

100g mixed fresh berries
20 fresh mint leaves

Jelly mould

1. Place the lemonade, Pimms, sugar and lemon juice in a pan and bring to a simmer. In the meantime, put the gelatine in ice cold water. Once the pan has come to the boil, remove from the heat.

2. Remove the gelatine from the water and squeeze out any excess water. Stir it slowly into the Pimms mixture until it's dissolved. Leave to cool slightly.

3. Pour a 10ml layer of the Pimms mixture into a jelly mould and put in the fridge to set.

4. While you're waiting for the jelly, quarter the cucumber lengthways and remove the seeds. Dice and place on kitchen paper to remove any excess moisture. Repeat this with the apple and grapefruit.

5. Place a layer of cucumber in the jelly mould. Pour in a little more jelly to cover and put back in the fridge to set. Repeat this process with the berries and mint, followed by the apple and grapefruit, and finally a mix of what's left. Chill until thoroughly set.

6. Turn the jelly out onto a large serving dish.

Summer Punch

Serves 10-12 20 mins preparation, 12 hours marinating

Ingredients

125g Demerara sugar
200ml water
2 star anise
½ cinnamon stick
1 bay leaf
4 cloves

750ml bottle rosé or
white wine
10 strawberries, halved
1 orange, sliced
1 lemon, sliced
Peel of 1 cucumber

6 sprigs mint
750ml lemonade or
Prosecco

Large glass jug

1. In a large pan, bring the sugar and water to the boil. Add the star anise, cinnamon, bay leaf and cloves and simmer for 5 minutes.

2. Add the wine. Cover and stand in a cool place for 12 hours.

3. To serve, pass the punch through a fine sieve into a large glass jug, and add all the fruit, cucumber and mint. Pour in the lemonade or Prosecco, stir and add ice cubes if you want it really chilled.

Summer Picnic Favourites

We always hope for a warm, sunny summer. If this year's weather encourages you to venture into the great outdoors, these recipes will help you enjoy it to the full. And even if rain stops play, there's enough comfort food here to keep you smiling.

Cornish and Vegetarian Pasties

Serves 6 40 mins preparation, 45 mins cooking

Ingredients

For the pastry	For the meat filling	For the vegetarian filling
335g plain flour	2 tablespoons vegetable oil	300g butternut squash, peeled and diced
½ teaspoon salt	1 onion, finely chopped	300g sweet potato, peeled and diced
75g lard or solid vegetable oil, diced	350g beef skirt or rump, diced	2 tablespoons sage, chopped
75g unsalted butter, diced	100ml beef stock	50g unsalted butter, diced
Very cold water to mix	150g swede, diced	Sea salt and milled black pepper
1 egg, beaten (for glaze)	1 medium potato, diced	200g Wensleydale cheese, crumbled
	1 sprig thyme, finely chopped	
	Sea salt and milled black pepper	

To make the pastry

1. Sieve the flour and salt into a large bowl, and add the lard or solid vegetable oil and butter straight from the fridge. Rub through your fingers lightly until you have a mixture resembling breadcrumbs. Add a little of the water and bring the mixture together. Knead lightly into a dough, wrap in cling film and refrigerate for 30 minutes.

For the meat filling

1. Pre-heat the oven to 200°C/gas mark 6.

2. Heat a large frying pan, add 1 tablespoon of the vegetable oil and the onion, and cook for 2-3 minutes. Remove from the pan and retain in a bowl. Re-heat the pan and once hot, add the remaining oil to seal the beef for 3-4 minutes. Then add to the onion.

3. Add the stock to the pan and reduce until you have 2-3 tablespoons. Pour over the beef and onion, and mix in the swede, potato and thyme.

4. On a lightly floured surface, roll the pastry into a 3mm thickness and cut 6 disks using a side plate as a template. Pile the filling equally in the centre of each circle of pastry and season with salt and pepper. Moisten half the pastry border with a little water, then bring 2 edges to meet on top of the filling. Pinch and twist the pastry firmly together to form a fluted ridge.

5. Grease a baking sheet, sprinkle with a tablespoon of water, and add the pasties. Using a fork, prick each side of the pasty and brush all over with the beaten egg.

6. Bake for 25 minutes, reduce the temperature to 150°C/gas mark 2 and cook for a further 20 minutes.

For the vegetarian filling

1. Pre-heat the oven to 200°C/gas mark 6.

2. Place the butternut squash, sweet potato and sage in the centre of a large sheet of tin foil. Add the butter, season with salt and pepper, crunch the foil together into a parcel and bake for 15 minutes.

3. Remove from the foil onto a plate and leave to cool.

4. Roll the pastry as above. Add the vegetarian filling in the same way and sprinkle the crumbled Wensleydale on top. Seal as above.

5. Bake for 20 minutes, reduce the temperature to 150°C/gas mark 2 and cook for a further 10 minutes.

Pork Pies

Pork Pies

We're all so used to buying pork pies that we don't realise how good they taste when we make them ourselves at home. They take a little time, but they're nearly as enjoyable to make as they are to eat!

Makes 8 individual pies 1 hour preparation, 1 hour 30 mins cooking

Ingredients
For the pastry
500g plain flour
1 teaspoon table salt
250ml water
175g lard
1 egg, beaten

For the filling
1kg boneless pork shoulder with 25% fat content, diced
200g rindless back bacon, diced
1 tablespoon sage, finely chopped
½ teaspoon ground nutmeg
½ teaspoon ground mace
1 onion, very finely chopped
Sea salt and milled black pepper

6.5cm pastry cutter

To make the filling

1. In a food processor, pulse the pork and bacon into small pieces, but don't mince it. Mix in the rest of the filling ingredients and divide into 8 equal amounts.

2. To make the filling into pie shapes, press each divided amount into a 6.5cm pastry cutter. Place them on a tray and refrigerate for 20 minutes.

To make the pastry

1. Sift the flour and salt into a large bowl.

2. In a pan, heat the water and lard. Bring to the boil, and pour onto the flour, stirring until you have a smooth pastry dough.

3. Put a quarter of the pastry to one side, and divide the rest into 8 equal amounts.

To finish the pies

1. Pre-heat the oven to 200°C/gas mark 6.

2. While the pastry is still warm, mould each of the 8 pieces into a large disc, using your fingers. Then mould each one around the base and sides of a portion of the pork filling.

3. Using the same method, divide the reserved quarter of pastry into 8, and mould into discs to form the pie lids.

4. Press the lids onto each pie, making sure they fit tightly to the sides, and brush all over with the beaten egg. Cut a small slit in each lid to release the steam.

5. Bake the pies for 30 minutes, then reduce the temperature to 150°C/gas mark 2 and bake for a further 45 minutes. Serve warm or cold.

Oak Roast Salmon Scotch Eggs

Making your own Scotch eggs is easier than it looks, so it's a great way to impress your guests. And replacing the traditional sausage meat with a tasty mixture of fresh and smoked salmon makes them even more memorable.

Serves 4 1 hour 10 mins preparation, 10 mins cooking

Ingredients

4 medium eggs	300g oak roast salmon
Sea salt and milled black pepper	1 egg, beaten
100g fresh salmon, diced	1 tablespoon milk
1 egg white	50g plain flour
1 teaspoon creamed horseradish sauce	100g breadcrumbs
1 tablespoon crème fraîche	1 litre vegetable oil

1. In a large pan of boiling salted water, boil the eggs for 5 minutes.

2. Put the pan in the sink under cold running water, until the eggs are cool.

3. Peel the eggs and keep to one side.

4. Purée the fresh salmon in a food processor. Add the egg white, pepper and horseradish sauce, then the crème fraîche, and pulse until combined into a mousse.

5. Flake the oak roast salmon away from the skin and place in a large bowl. Add the salmon mousse and mix together.

6. In a separate bowl, mix the beaten egg with the milk. Put the flour in a second bowl, and the breadcrumbs in a third.

7. Take one of the peeled eggs and roll it in the flour.

8. In the palm of your hand, take a quarter of the salmon mixture and flatten it into a disk shape. Add the egg to the centre and roll the salmon mixture around the egg, so it's evenly covered.

9. Repeat this process with the remaining 3 eggs, then put them all in the fridge for 20 minutes to set.

10. Remove the eggs from the fridge. Then, roll each egg in the flour, dip into the beaten egg and finally roll in the breadcrumbs to complete your scotch eggs. Put them in the fridge for another 20 minutes.

11. In a large pan, heat the vegetable oil and deep fry 2 eggs at a time for 4-5 minutes until golden brown. Serve warm or cold.

Oak Roast Salmon Scotch Eggs

Classic Cream Tea

Classic Cream Tea

For the perfect English afternoon tea, you can't beat homemade scones with jam and clotted cream. These are very straightforward to make, and go perfectly with my raspberry jam.

Makes 12 scones 20 mins preparation, 15 mins cooking

Ingredients
450g self-raising flour
½ teaspoon baking powder
1 pinch salt
100g cold, unsalted butter, diced
75g caster sugar
75g sultanas
1 large egg
225ml milk

6.5cm pastry cutter

To serve
Clotted cream
Raspberry jam (see page 90 for my recipe)

1. Pre-heat the oven to 200°C/gas mark 6.

2. Sift the flour, baking powder and salt into a large mixing bowl.

3. Add the butter and rub it into the flour using your fingers, until the mixture resembles breadcrumbs. Mix in the sugar and sultanas.

4. In a separate bowl, beat the egg and stir in the milk. Pour two thirds of this into the scone mixture, stirring constantly until the dough comes together. The consistency should be firm but moist, so add more milk and egg if you need to.

5. Place the dough onto a lightly floured surface and knead to bring it together, but don't overwork the dough. Roll out to a 2cm thickness.

6. Use a 6.5cm pastry cutter dipped in flour to cut out 12 scones, and place them on a baking sheet.

7. Brush the tops with the remaining milk and egg mixture, and bake for 15 minutes until risen and lightly golden.

8. Serve as soon as possible with clotted cream and raspberry jam.

Homemade Lemonade and Summer Pimms

Homemade Lemonade

Really refreshing and zingy, this is the perfect way to wash down a summer picnic – or simply enjoy on its own while you're relaxing in the sun.

Makes 1.5 litres 15 mins preparation, plus cooling time

Ingredients
5 large unwaxed lemons
125g caster sugar
1.2 litres boiling water

1.5 litre sterilised bottle

1. Wash 2 of the lemons, then remove the zest using a potato peeler or sharp knife, being careful to leave all the pith (white part) behind.

2. Squeeze the juice from all the lemons and place in a bowl with the zest. Mix in the sugar.

3. Add the boiling water, stir well to make sure the sugar dissolves, and leave to cool.

4. When it's cool, check the sweetness and add more sugar if you need to.

5. Pour the lemonade through a coarse sieve to remove the zest and pips, then pour into the sterilised bottle. Keep in the fridge until you need it and serve with fresh mint.

Summer Pimms

The fruit, mint and lemonade are every bit as important to this drink as the Pimms itself – and the secret to recreating the authentic British summer tipple.

Serves 6 10 mins preparation

Ingredients
250ml Pimms
1 litre lemonade
1 cucumber, sliced
1 apple, cored and chopped

1 orange, sliced
3 strawberries, sliced
½ lime, sliced
Handful of fresh mint

Large glass jug

1. Pour the Pimms into a large glass jug.

2. Add the lemonade and all the other ingredients.

3. Serve with plenty of ice.

Barbecue

That chargrilled taste lends itself to so much more than straightforward sausages and burgers. If you're looking for something different to 'throw on the barbie', here's where you'll find it.

Tiger Prawn Skewers on Toast

Tiger Prawn Skewers on Toast

Sweet, juicy tiger prawns work perfectly with garlic and chilli. A touch of fresh lemon balances their richness, and the toast soaks up all the lovely juices.

Serves 4 25 mins preparation, 10 mins cooking

Ingredients
36 uncooked tiger prawns
1 tablespoon sea salt
4 cloves garlic, crushed
1 pinch dried chilli flakes
1 pinch medium curry powder
6 slices white country bread
150g unsalted butter
Juice of 1 lemon
1 tablespoon parsley, finely chopped

12 small wooden skewers

1. In a bowl, mix the prawns and sea salt, and leave to marinade for 5 minutes – this helps bring out the sweetness of the prawns.

2. Wash off the salt under cold running water, and pat the prawns dry on kitchen paper.

3. In another bowl, mix the garlic, chilli flakes and curry powder. Add the prawns, coating them in the mixture, then thread 3 onto each skewer.

4. While you heat a large frying pan, toast the slices of bread lightly and keep in a warm place.

5. When the pan's hot, add the butter, quickly followed by the prawn skewers. Keep turning the skewers for 4-5 minutes, until the prawns turn a nice pink colour. Add the lemon juice and parsley.

6. Place a slice of toast in the centre of each plate, cross 3 skewers over, and drizzle with the pan juices.

Beer Can Chicken

This recipe may sound a little strange – and the chicken does look funny perched on a beer can – but it gives you fantastically moist meat. The marinade creates a wonderful depth of flavour too.

Serves 4-6 15 mins preparation, 50 mins cooking, 3 hours marinating

Ingredients
1.8kg free range chicken
Sea salt and milled black pepper
500ml can light golden ale

Barbecue with a lid
Large foil tray

For the Marinade
100ml tomato ketchup
1 tablespoon soft dark brown sugar
1 teaspoon ground coriander
1 teaspoon ground cumin
1 teaspoon smoked paprika
1 clove garlic, crushed

To make the marinade

1. Combine all the marinade ingredients.

2. Place the chicken in a large bowl, season with salt and pepper and coat thoroughly with the marinade mixture.

3. Leave to marinade for 2 hours in the fridge, and then for 1 hour at room temperature while you light the barbecue.

To cook the chicken

1. When the coals are covered with white ash, carefully move them to the sides of the barbecue and place a large foil tray in the centre to use as a drip tray.

2. Empty half the beer from the can, then carefully place the chicken onto the can so it's sitting upright with the can in its cavity.

3. Place the chicken on the barbecue above the drip tray. Cover with the barbecue lid and cook for 50 minutes.

4. Remove the chicken from the barbecue and rest for 15 minutes before carving.

If you prefer, you can roast the chicken in an oven at 190°C/gas mark 5 using the same beer can method.

Beer Can Chicken

Sticky Ribs

Spicy, sweet and succulent, these ribs are packed with flavour. The marinade is so much better than any shop-bought barbecue sauce – and really easy, as long as you remember to plan ahead.

Serves 6 15 mins preparation, at least 5 hours marinating, 1 hour cooking

Ingredients

2 tablespoons sesame seed oil
4 tablespoons soy sauce
3 tablespoons tomato ketchup
3 tablespoons clear honey
2 tablespoons sweet chilli sauce
1 orange, juice and grated zest

2 cloves garlic, crushed
30g fresh root ginger, grated
1 star anise, ground
1 teaspoon smoked paprika
1.5kg spare ribs

1. Combine all the ingredients to make a marinade.

2. In a large bowl, coat the ribs in the marinade. Cover and keep in the fridge for at least 5 hours.

3. Pre-heat the oven to 200°C/gas mark 6.

4. Line a roasting tin with foil, add the ribs and roast for 1 hour, turning them from time to time.

5. Serve immediately, or leave to cool and reheat on a barbecue.

Sticky Ribs

Halloumi Cheese Skewers with Aubergine Dip

Halloumi Cheese Skewers with Aubergine Dip

Serves 4 40 mins preparation, 45 mins cooking

Ingredients
For the Skewers

225g Halloumi cheese, diced
2 tablespoons olive oil
1 teaspoon fresh thyme leaves
1 large red pepper
1 large yellow pepper
1 bulb fennel
1 red onion
1 punnet cherry tomatoes

For the Aubergine Dip

2 aubergines
1 tablespoon sea salt
3 tablespoons virgin olive oil
1 teaspoon ground cumin
6 cloves garlic
2 sprigs thyme
2 tablespoons tahini paste
Juice of 1 lemon
125ml Greek-style yogurt
1 tablespoon coriander, chopped

To serve

Flat breads

8 wooden skewers

To make the dip

1. Pre-heat oven to 190°C/gas mark 5.

2. Cut the aubergines in half and criss-cross the flesh using a pointed knife.

3. Scatter the sea salt in the centre of a large sheet of baking foil. Place the aubergines on top, skin side down, and drizzle with 2 tablespoons of olive oil. Dust with ground cumin, then add the garlic and sprigs of thyme.

4. Bring the sides of the foil together and fold to make a sealed parcel. Place on a baking tray and bake for 30 minutes, until the aubergines are soft.

5. When they're cool enough to handle, use a spoon to scoop the flesh from the aubergines and place in a food processor. Peel the garlic and add it to the aubergine flesh, along with the tahini paste and lemon juice. Blend until smooth.

6. Spoon the mixture into a bowl. When it's cool, fold in the yogurt and coriander, and taste to check if it needs a little more salt. Spoon the dip into a serving bowl, and drizzle it with the remaining olive oil.

To make the skewers

1. Place the halloumi in a bowl with the olive oil and the thyme leaves. Leave it to marinade while you prepare the peppers.

2. De-seed the peppers and cut them into 2cm square pieces. Cut the fennel and onion into similar shape and size pieces. Thread a cherry tomato onto each skewer, followed by pieces of red and yellow pepper, cheese, fennel and onion. Repeat until the skewers are full.

To cook and serve the skewers

1. When the charcoal has turned white, cook the skewers for 10-12 minutes, turning occasionally. Make sure the flames don't touch the skewers. If you prefer, you can brush the skewers with a little olive oil and cook them under a grill or on a heated griddle pan.

2. Serve with the aubergine dip and flat breads.

Barbecued Spiced Peaches

When you've finished cooking the main course on your barbecue, the coals will probably stay hot for quite a while – and this easy summer dessert is a tasty way to make the most of the heat.

Serves 4 **15 mins preparation, 30 mins cooking**

Ingredients
4 fresh ripe peaches
2 tablespoons soft brown sugar
4 tablespoons rum
20g unsalted butter, diced
1 vanilla pod, split lengthways
1 cinnamon stick
2 star anise

To serve
Vanilla ice cream or double cream

1. Cut the peaches in half, remove the stones and place each half, skin side down, in the centre of a large sheet of baking foil.

2. Sprinkle the sugar and rum evenly over the peaches, and dot with the butter.

3. Add the vanilla, cinnamon and star anise, then bring the sides of the foil together and fold to create a sealed parcel.

4. Cook on a barbecue for 30 minutes, or cook in the oven at 180°C/gas mark 4 for 20 minutes.

5. Serve with vanilla ice cream or double cream.

Barbecued Spiced Peaches

Spiced Lamb Koftas with Roasted Aubergine

Spiced Lamb Koftas with Roasted Aubergine

These sausage-shaped kebabs are packed with interesting flavours. They're simple to make, as it's mainly just a case of combining all the ingredients.

Serves 4 25 mins preparation, 30 mins cooking

Ingredients

500g prime minced lamb
1 large red onion, finely chopped
2 cloves garlic, crushed
2 tablespoons fresh coriander, chopped
1 teaspoon dried chilli flakes
2 teaspoons ground cumin
1 teaspoon ground coriander
½ teaspoon ground cinnamon
1 teaspoon smoked paprika
Sea salt and milled black pepper

2 aubergines
6 tablespoons olive oil

To serve
Coriander
350g houmous
200g tzatziki
1 lemon, cut into wedges

12 wooden skewers

1. Pre-heat the oven to 180°C/gas mark 4.

2. In a bowl, bind the lamb, onion, garlic, coriander and all the spices, and season with salt and pepper.

3. Using wet hands, shape the mixture into 12 sausage shapes. (You can cover these and leave them in the fridge for up to 24 hours until you're ready to cook them.)

4. Remove the top and bottom of the aubergines and cut each one into 4 equal, thick slices. Use a pointed knife to score the flesh on both sides.

5. Heat a frying pan, add 3 tablespoons of olive oil and fry the aubergines until golden on each side. Season them with sea salt and roast in the oven for 15 minutes.

6. Heat a large frying pan, add a little olive oil and fry the koftas for 5 minutes until brown on each side. Place in the oven and cook for a further 10 minutes.

7. Remove the koftas from the oven and keep in a warm place. When they're cool enough to handle, push a skewer through the length of each kofta.

8. Scatter the koftas with coriander. Serve alongside the roasted aubergine, houmous, tzatziki and lemon wedges.

Coleslaw

I add fennel and apple to my coleslaw to give it a burst of freshness, a hint of sweetness and plenty of satisfying crunch. It's the perfect accompaniment to most barbecued food – and difficult to resist on its own!

Serves 6 20 mins preparation

Ingredients
½ firm, white cabbage, cored
1 bulb fennel, quartered and cored
1 granny smith apple, quartered and cored
2 large carrots, peeled

2 tablespoons milk
6 tablespoons mayonnaise
Juice of ½ lemon
Sea salt and milled black pepper

1. Using a mandolin or sharp knife, shred the cabbage and fennel as finely as possible.

2. Grate the apple and the carrots.

3. In a large mixing bowl, whisk together the milk, mayonnaise and lemon juice, and season with salt and pepper.

4. Fold in the rest of the ingredients and place into a serving dish.

Potato Salad

Of all the potato dishes, this is my favourite for the summer. The combination of waxy new potatoes, spring onions and mayonnaise is a winner with all kinds of salads – and, of course, with a barbecue.

Serves 6 20 mins preparation, 25 mins cooking

Ingredients
1kg small new potatoes
6 tablespoons mayonnaise
3 tablespoons milk
Sea salt and milled black pepper

1 pinch paprika
2 shallots, peeled and finely chopped
4 spring onions, finely sliced
Small bunch chives, finely chopped

1. Put the new potatoes into a pan of salted water, bring to the boil and simmer for 20-25 minutes until tender.

2. Chill under cold running water and peel if necessary.

3. In a large bowl, mix the mayonnaise, milk, salt, pepper and paprika.

4. Cut the potatoes into quarters and add to the mayonnaise mixture, along with the shallots, spring onions and chives. Bind everything together, taste to check the seasoning, and serve.

Coleslaw and Potato Salad

Cherished Preserves & Condiments

When fresh fruit and vegetables are in abundance, it's time to bottle some of that goodness to enjoy all year round. With these recipes, you have a lasting taste of summer.

Raspberry Jam

Makes 5 x 450ml jars 20 mins preparation, 30-35 mins cooking

Ingredients
1.3kg preserving sugar (or granulated sugar)
1.3kg fresh raspberries
5 sterilised jam jars (450ml) with wax discs and cellophane tops

1. Pre-heat the oven to 180°C/gas mark 4.

2. Put the sugar in an ovenproof bowl and place in the oven.

3. Put 3 small plates in the freezer – you'll need these to test if the jam is setting.

4. Put the raspberries in a heavy-bottomed pan and simmer on a low to medium heat until the juices start to run – this will take about 10 minutes. You can stir occasionally, but try not to break up all the fruit.

5. Remove the sugar from the oven and add to the raspberries. Stir gently until the sugar is completely dissolved.

6. Turn the heat up to maximum and boil the jam rapidly for 5 minutes. Remove any scum that forms on the surface.

7. Take the pan off the heat, and spoon a little of the jam onto one of the plates from the freezer. Allow it to cool, then push it with your finger to see if the surface wrinkles. If it does, it has set. If not, boil the jam for a further 5 minutes and test again.

8. Once you've achieved the set, leave the jam for 5-10 minutes before pouring it into the sterilised jars.

9. Place a wax disc on top of each one while it's still hot, and seal with the cellophane tops. Leave to cool before labelling. Jam keeps for 6-8 months unopened.

Lemon Curd

Makes 1 x 300ml jar 20 mins preparation, 20 mins cooking

Ingredients
150g caster sugar
2 eggs

2 unwaxed lemons, juice and grated zest
50g unsalted butter, diced
1 sterilised jar (300ml) with wax discs and cellophane tops

1. Place a bowl over a pan of barely simmering water, ensuring the water doesn't touch the base of the bowl. Add the sugar to the bowl.

2. Beat the eggs well, then add the lemon juice and zest. Add this mixture to the sugar, along with the butter.

3. Stir continuously for 20 minutes, until the mixture thickens and becomes smooth.

4. Spoon the lemon curd into a sterilised jar. Lemon curd keeps for 6-8 months unopened.

Raspberry Jam and Lemon Curd

Piccalilli and Pickled Beetroot

Piccalilli

Makes 3 x 300ml jars 25 mins preparation, 12 hours resting, 15 mins cooking

Ingredients

500g cauliflower, broken into small florets
200g pickling onions, peeled and chopped
100g cucumber, de-seeded and diced
200g runner beans, topped, tailed and cut
into 2cm lengths diagonally
100g courgettes, topped, tailed and diced
100g carrots, peeled and diced
2 tablespoons table salt
1 tablespoon turmeric
50g mustard powder

2 teaspoons ground ginger
50g plain flour
¼ teaspoon nutmeg
½ teaspoon cayenne pepper
5 tablespoons cider vinegar plus 150ml
250ml malt vinegar
2 tablespoons water

3 300ml sterilised jars

1. Place the prepared vegetables in a large bowl, add the salt, then cover and leave for a minimum of 12 hours. The salt will draw out the liquid giving a more intense flavour.

2. In a large saucepan, mix the turmeric, mustard, ginger, flour, nutmeg and cayenne pepper with the 5 tablespoons of cider vinegar. Slowly add the rest of the cider vinegar, vegetables, malt vinegar and water.

3. Gently heat the mixture until it thickens and keep stirring. This will take about 15 minutes. Do not over boil as the vegetables will lose their crunch.

4. Carefully ladle into sterilised jars, cover and keep until required. They will keep for 6 months if unopened, and 4 weeks in the fridge once opened.

Pickled Beetroot

Makes 1 x 500ml jar 15 mins preparation, 3 hours 30 mins cooking

Ingredients

450g raw beetroot, washed
2 tablespoon sea salt
2 shallots, peeled and thinly sliced

175ml balsamic vinegar
½ teaspoon dried chilli
1 500ml sterilised jar

1. Pre-heat the oven to 190°C/gas mark 5.

2. Trim the beetroot but leave the skins on. Add the sea salt to the centre of a large sheet of tin foil, place the beetroot on top and secure the edges of the foil into a parcel. Bake for 2 ½ hours until they feel tender when pierced with a skewer.

3. Remove the beetroot from the oven and as soon as it is cool enough to handle, remove the skins before slicing thinly.

4. Layer the sliced beetroot and shallots into the sterilised jar.

5. Put the vinegar and chilli into a small saucepan and bring to a simmer. Pour over the beetroot and shallots to cover them completely and seal the jar.

6. Leave for a couple of days before using, or keep for 6 months unopened.

Lamona Appliance, Sink and Tap Collection

The Lamona range is exclusive to Howdens Joinery and has been selected to perfectly complement our range of kitchens.

Lamona appliances are designed to look great and are manufactured to the highest standards to ensure they are durable and reliable, use less energy and water, and run quietly, whilst providing excellent value for money.

You can choose from ovens, microwave ovens, hobs, extractors, fridges, freezers, dishwashers, washing machines, tumble dryers, sinks and taps, which are all designed to fit beautifully in your Howdens kitchen.

All Lamona appliances come with a 2 year manufacturer's guarantee and what we believe is the best after sales service in the UK.

You will have the reassurance that we supply 500,000 appliances and 600,000 sinks and taps each year to UK homes.

Lamona is available from stock in over 500 local depots to your trade professional. To find out more and for detailed product specifications, please refer to **www.lamona.co.uk**

The General Tarleton

An old coaching inn with contemporary comforts, The General Tarleton Inn is in the pretty village of Ferrensby close to both York and Harrogate. Owned and run by John and Claire Topham for the past 12 years, The General Tarleton is constantly evolving but always sticks to the basic philosophy of offering great service and excellent food and drink in a relaxed atmosphere, and if you are staying the night, a comfortable room to rest your head.

The focus is on food

In The General Tarleton kitchen, John heads an experienced and dedicated team. Menus change daily to reflect the seasons and the pick of the catch or crop that day. John gets a call most days from the fishing boats as they return to port and within hours the fish is in the kitchen. Yorkshire has an abundance of excellent suppliers which The General Tarleton has worked with over the years to obtain the very best seasonal produce.

The General Tarleton Inn, Boroughbridge Road, Ferrensby, Knaresborough, HG5 0PZ
Tel 01423 340284 www.generaltarleton.co.uk